DON’T
QUIT

DON'T QUIT

Text by Abi McMahon

An Hachette UK Company
www.hachette.co.uk

Vie Books, an imprint of Summersdale Publishers Ltd
Part of Octopus Publishing Group Limited
Carmelite House
50 Victoria Embankment
LONDON
EC4Y 0DZ
UK

www.summersdale.com

Printed and bound in China

ISBN: 978-1-78685-774-3

DON'T QUIT

HOW TO KICK-START YOUR PLANS AND MAKE THE MOST OF YOUR TIME

Hal Fisher

INTRODUCTION

THE FIRST STEP TO SUCCESS IS TRYING

I HAVE THE COURAGE TO TAKE THE FIRST STEP ON MY JOURNEY.

Every success story has one thing in common: they all started with day one. When you have the courage to try, you take the same first step as anyone who has ever succeeded. The journey to achieving something will hold challenges, but you'll learn something about yourself every time you overcome one.

Knowing where to start can be tricky, but there are lots of simple ways to maximize your planning, organization, focus, resilience and fortitude. The tips and advice in this book will help you to start, continue and persevere, whatever your endeavour.

You can, you should, and if you're brave enough to start, you will.

Stephen King

PART ONE

MOTIVATION AND DISCIPLINE

I AM MOTIVATED TO START AND I HAVE THE DISCIPLINE TO CONTINUE.

How many of us have quit before we've even started? Sadly, it's easier to talk yourself out of things than into things; easy to follow your self-doubt and ignore your desire to change things for the better. This is why starting something really is a big achievement.

The inspiration to get started is motivation, but the ability to continue comes from discipline. They may be mistaken for the same thing but are in fact very different; however, when paired they make a winning formula.

THERE WILL BE OBSTACLES. THERE WILL BE DOUBTERS. THERE WILL BE MISTAKES. BUT WITH HARD WORK, THERE ARE NO LIMITS.

Michael Phelps

SET THE DATE

Decide a date for when you will start your new endeavour. Write what you plan to do on your calendar and say to yourself, "On this day I will start doing X." Seeing it written down and hearing yourself say it out loud will move your idea from your head into the real world. If you need even more of a push, decide what time would be best to start and set a reminder on your phone or watch.

Make sure you don't accept any invitations for the day you set, and clear your schedule as much as you can. Then, when the day comes, start your new endeavour.

NO DAY SPENT
IN PURSUIT OF
MY DREAM IS A
DAY WASTED.

START SMALL

Sometimes the problem isn't that you don't have enough drive to do something but that you have too much. It's easy to put all your time into starting something new and then burn out, letting the project drop by the wayside because you are tired or want to reclaim some of your time. Or, you may feel overwhelmed by all the things you want to do and not know where to start.

Start small while you are forming your new routine so you are better able to sustain it. Complete one task and stop while you are still excited or have the energy to do more. Your excitement will fuel your motivation, which will in turn keep you returning to your activity and assist in the forming of a habit.

Don’t loaf and invite inspiration; light out after it with a club.

Jack London

HOW MUCH TIME DO YOU HAVE TO SPARE?

You may wonder where you'll find the time to dedicate to working toward your goal. First, think about how much time it would take to contribute meaningfully to your new project on a regular basis: is it something that can be done in sharp ten-minute bursts or do you need at least an hour each time for it to have a significant effect? Next, look for places in your schedule where you can find this chunk of "project time" and book it in on your calendar.

If you only need a short amount of time, why not spend some of your lunch break working toward your goal, or get up 20 minutes earlier than usual to get ideas going before you've even started your day? And if you need a bigger time slot, try booking evenings of "project time" a week ahead, so that it takes priority over less productive or frivolous ways you would usually fill your evenings – such as scrolling through social media or mindlessly binging a box set.

I WILL CONGRATULATE MYSELF WITH EVERY STEP I TAKE TOWARD ACHIEVING MY DREAM.

THE **BEST** TIME
TO START IS
NOW.

Never give up, have the passion. Don’t be afraid.

Barbara Broccoli

YOU MAY HAVE TO CREATE YOUR OWN MOTIVATION

Sometimes you want to undertake a new project because you are excited about the challenges it holds as well as the end result. Sometimes you would like to achieve the end result, but you are not stimulated by the steps you will have to take to get there. This is particularly true of goals based on self-improvement such as “getting fit”. We know the end result will be good, but if we enjoyed the process we would already be doing it!

In these situations it can be useful to add motivation to your process. This can be as simple as writing yourself a list of tasks that you can cross off as you go or awarding yourself stickers for each milestone you achieve. Perhaps you could put a small amount of money to one side, to access only when you hit a milestone.

IT DOES NOT MATTER
HOW SLOWLY YOU GO
SO LONG AS YOU DO
NOT STOP.

Confucius

IT TAKES X AMOUNT OF TIMES TO FORM A HABIT

Research by University College London showed that it takes, on average, around 66 days for most routines to become habit. However, crucially, it found that the harder the habit, the longer it took to form *and* that some people simply didn't find habit-forming easy and therefore they would form habits on a longer timescale.

Take it easy on yourself. Don't worry about missing one day here and there when establishing your new routine (the same study found that this did not materially affect the development of a habit) and don't worry if it is taking you longer to get into your new routine than you think it should – the important thing is that you are *on your way* to building a new habit.

It does not matter if I am not progressing at the same speed as others as long as I am progressing.

The man who removes a mountain begins by carrying away small stones.

Chinese proverb

ADD A LITTLE NOTHING INTO YOUR DAY

Now that you've adjusted your schedule to allow for the time you're going to spend on your new project, find an extra ten minutes to do nothing. For that ten minutes just sit and be idle. Perhaps you could spend this time preparing yourself mentally for the challenge ahead, or just mulling over your project.

A study published in *Psychological Science* found that a daily dose of doing "nothing" actually increases your productivity and makes you more likely to commit to a certain goal. Allowing yourself ten minutes of downtime to be mindful and restore your energy will make you more effective when you actually get down to work.

BE FIRM YET FLEXIBLE

You will have good days and bad days, and discipline is finding a way to persevere regardless of what kind of day you are having. Set yourself an upper time budget and a lower time budget so you can flex your schedule around the realities of your life.

The upper time budget is for the good days, so you can take advantage of days when you have plenty of energy and enthusiasm and do a little more without burning yourself out. The lower time budget is for days when you are tired or down. It may be less time than you think you need, and it might not make a huge contribution to your project, but doing at least something, however little, toward your project will help you to form your routine.

COMPLETING A TASK IS MUCH EASIER WHEN IT IS A HABIT.

I AVOID LOOKING FORWARD OR BACKWARD, AND TRY TO KEEP LOOKING UPWARD.

Charlotte Brontë

SET A MEASURABLE TARGET

Some projects have inbuilt targets and measures of progress that make it easy to judge when you have reached them. For example, if the reason you picked up this book is to motivate yourself to change jobs, then you will have achieved that when you get a new job. Other endeavours, such as becoming a tidier person or learning a new language, are harder to parse.

If you are working toward something like learning a new skill, set yourself targets so you still benefit from the pleasurable sense of achievement. They could be things such as “I will always wash up dirty dishes within one hour of using them” or “I will be able to say at least five sentences in another language”.

It is as important to recognize the things I've done well as it is the things I need to improve upon.

INTRINSIC AND EXTRINSIC MOTIVATION

Intrinsic motivation is internal motivation. It is when a person is driven to achieve a goal for its own sake and feels that the completion of the goal is its own reward.

Extrinsic motivation is motivation driven by an external reward. An example of this might be practising your baking in order to win a baking competition.

Research shows that extrinsic motivation works well to inspire shorter bursts of productivity, while intrinsic motivation is the most effective in driving your long-term goals.

REMOVE TEMPTATIONS

Motivation may be how you get started, but discipline is the fuel that helps you to continue. When you are disciplined you are able to be as productive on the low-energy, reluctant days as you are on the easy days.

Help kick-start your discipline by removing temptations on the days you have allocated to work on your project. First, identify what it is that pulls you away from focussing on the tasks you'd like to tackle: do you keep checking your social media? Is your schedule too busy? Are you finding it too easy to veg out on the sofa? Then, create an obstacle between you and the distraction. Perhaps you could turn off your device and keep it in a drawer for the evening, or download an app designed to limit the time you spend on certain time-draining websites. Maybe it would be a good idea to mark certain days on your calendar as "busy" or message your friends and family members to say you're unavailable. Consider going to a neutral space, such as a library or a café, where your distractions can't reach you.

IF I AM STRUGGLING, I WILL BE MY OWN BEST HELPER.

GETTING IN THE RIGHT MINDSET

Being in the right headspace is important if you're going to get your best work done. When you settle down to work, try some quick wins to get your motivation flowing.

Remind yourself why you're doing this. Think back to the moment you decided to undertake this task – if you can relive that moment of inspiration, you may be able to harness the ambition and drive you felt when you started. Remember the good reason you're embarking on this project – whether it is going to create something that helps people, or it will make you a better person – and focus your mind on that, rather than on the steps you will have to take to get there.

Finally, close your eyes and picture yourself achieving your goal. Really try to embody the "future you" – think about how good it will feel to tick off every task along the way, and the satisfaction you'll feel when you reach your goal. Let that be your inspiration.

You must do the thing you think you cannot do.

Eleanor Roosevelt

PART TWO

PREPARATION AND PLANNING

I MAY NOT EXPECT IT, BUT I AM PREPARED FOR IT.

Spend some time thinking about how you work best, and you will give yourself an incredible head start on achieving your goals. If you work in a way that's tailor-made to suit your personality traits, then you are less likely to struggle, and less likely to quit.

This does take a little trial and error and research on what techniques are out there. This chapter looks at the different ways you can break down tasks and how you might adapt working techniques to suit your preferences.

Someone is sitting in the shade today because someone planted a tree a long time ago.

Warren Buffett

I DARE TO
DREAM AND
I PLAN TO
ACHIEVE.

A LITTLE LIST IS A LOT OF HELP

Make a “to-do-next-time” list at the end of every session you spend working toward your goal. Include at least one concrete, achievable goal or incomplete task for you to tackle the next time you work on your project. Planning while everything is fresh in your mind will cut unfocused time from your next session.

The concrete goal could be something like “Run 5k” or “Finish this section”. Write it on a notepad and cross it off when you have achieved it.

I'VE LEARNED IT'S IMPORTANT NOT TO LIMIT YOURSELF. YOU CAN DO WHATEVER YOU REALLY LOVE TO DO, NO MATTER WHAT IT IS.

Ryan Gosling

IF SOMETHING ISN'T WORKING, THEN I HAVE THE POWER TO CHANGE IT.

PLAN B IS STILL A PLAN

Sometimes things go wrong, and that's OK! Set aside some time to plan ahead for what you will do if you aren't going to hit the deadline you have set yourself. Keep things hypothetical and don't spend too much time worrying about *why* things might go wrong – that doesn't matter – and instead simply set your next-best target.

For example, you may be aiming to complete a craft project to give for someone's birthday. Decide whether, if you do find yourself behind on your deadline, you would prefer to schedule in more sessions to complete the task by the deadline or if you would prefer to adjust the delivery date – even if that means writing an IOU to your friend. Should this problem then arise you will have already made the tricky decision, in less stressful circumstances.

When something really matters, you should never give up or give in.

Gordon Brown

I AM FLEXIBLE
AND CAN
ADAPT TO NEW
CIRCUMSTANCES.

USE THE "IF-THEN" TECHNIQUE

The "if-then" technique is designed to help you to figure out the ways in which your habits let you down and cause you to quit, and then to replace them with a concrete, positive action. The first thing to do is to scrutinize your habits and identify your problem. Perhaps you avoid doing your least favourite work on your project, but you can't proceed until it is done. For example, if you're looking to buy a house, perhaps you hate calling back estate agents or doing background research and technical planning.

The next stage is to identify a trigger that will definitely occur, such as a time or an action. This is your "if". Finally, connect the two: "**If** it is lunchtime, **then** I will call the estate agent" or "**If** I have sat down on the sofa, **then** I will research X for ten minutes". Setting a trigger causes your brain to link the two actions, resulting in you moving on to the dreaded task almost before you realize it!

IT IS BETTER
TO FORGE A
PATH AROUND
AN OBSTACLE
THAN IT IS TO
TRY TO BREAK
THROUGH IT.

WHEN ARE YOU AT YOUR BEST?

You have more freedom than you might think. You may be completing tasks at the "normal" time, but is it the best time for you? Experiment with the times when you tackle your project, and choose to work on it when you are at your best. Perhaps your fitness routine is to hit the gym straight after work, but you've actually achieved your best results when you've gone at 6 a.m., before breakfast. Maybe your words flow more freely late at night, so that might be the best time for you to write your job application.

Once you have identified your best time to work, use that knowledge to your advantage. You may not always be able to work on your project at the time that is best for you; your gym may only have two early-opening days a week or it may look odd to send in a job application at midnight. Instead, use your best time to do your best work. Schedule in your hardest workouts for the early-opening days or write your covering letter at midnight but submit the application in your lunch hour.

UNFORESEEN EVENTS CAN BE POSITIVE AS WELL AS NEGATIVE.

DON'T COUNT THE DAYS; MAKE THE DAYS COUNT.

Muhammad Ali

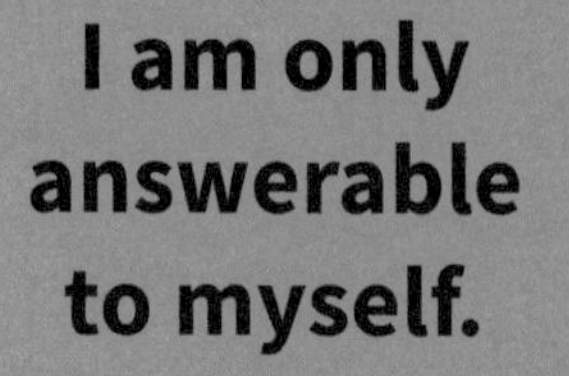
I am only
answerable
to myself.

A PRODUCTIVE WORKSPACE

Having a positive and conducive space to work in can make or break a project. Turn your project space into an oasis of calm to help you to be as productive as possible. Keep the space clean and clear, but with all the things you need to do your work to hand. Studies show that having plants in the room makes workers more productive – and it brightens the space and filters the air you're breathing to make sure you're on top form. Having photos or inspirational quotes around your space can also be a helpful reminder of what you're working toward.

Whatever you do, make sure your workspace is somewhere you want to spend time in and you'll find working on your project feels less like a chore.

The more I want to get something done, the less I call it work.

Richard Bach

CREATE A MOOD BOARD

Have you got a goal in mind, but you're not quite sure what it will entail? Or perhaps you just want a way to help you better visualize your goal and turn it from a dream into something more concrete? A mood board can help you to work out the details, as well as being an ever-evolving reminder of your dream and a source of stimulation along the way.

Make a physical mood board with a large sheet of paper or a scrapbook and images cut out from magazines or printed from the internet, along with your own drawings and notes to help you to work out what you want to achieve and what that may look like.

Sites such as Pinterest help you to do this in a neater way if you prefer to keep things in digital form – and you can "pin" things like articles, motivational talks from YouTube and inspirational quotes to your mood board, too. Experiment with what works best for you, and refer back to your mood board whenever you want a shot of instant motivation!

IT IS BETTER TO COMPLETE YOUR JOB TO A HIGH STANDARD THAN IT IS TO HAVE THE APPEARANCE OF "DOING IT ALL".

KNOWING YOUR ABCDs

If feeling overwhelmed by your project is causing you to consider quitting, implement a method of categorizing and prioritizing your workload. The ABCD technique groups your tasks into four categories, which helps you to know where to start:

A – **Tasks that are both urgent and important**
B – **Tasks that are important but not urgent**
C – **Tasks that are urgent but not important**
D – **Tasks that are not important and not urgent**

This may sound like an obvious way to prioritize tasks but it can help you to stop and question your feeling of "I have so much to do" to discover what really needs your attention and what can wait.

I AM IN CHARGE OF MY TIME AND I CHOOSE WHERE TO START.

PART THREE

SELF-BELIEF

I BELIEVE I CAN
AND SO I WILL.

We humans really can be our own worst enemy. Our brains can decide that we can't do something, even when all evidence points to the fact that not only *can* we do it, we *are* doing it!

But, you know, you don't have to listen to the negative voice in your head. Shore up your self-esteem and appreciate your achievements and you'll be able to ignore the doubts that are calling for you to quit. Don't be your own hater – be your own biggest cheerleader!

Doubt whom you will, but never yourself.

Christian Nestell Bovee

MY PURPOSE IS MEANINGFUL AND I SHOULD PURSUE IT.

INTERROGATE YOUR NEGATIVE THOUGHTS

Negative thoughts often stem from insecurities and are driven by emotion, and simply do not stand up to close scrutiny. The next time you think something negative about yourself, stop and ask "Why? What do I think I have done wrong?" If you cannot think of anything specific then recognize that this is not a true reflection of yourself and let go of the thought.

If you do identify a problem, then ask yourself "Is this true?" Write down a list of evidence that supports and disproves your bad thought. You'll often find that when you move your thoughts from your head to paper, your negative "reasoning" seems small and does not stand up to your positive attributes.

Another way to force negative thoughts into the light, where they lose their power, is to simply recognize that they are there. Recognize them for what they are: not an accurate take on your current situation but the voice of insecurity. Say to yourself "That is a negative thought. I recognize it and now I let it go" and then let it float out of your head.

I am strong,
able and
ready for the
challenges
I face.

FIND POSITIVE ROLE MODELS

Sometimes, no matter how prepared we are and how much planning and hard work we put in to a project, we can still have moments when we feel lost and uninspired. Having some positive role models to buoy you up at these times can be the difference between giving up and getting back on track. Seek out people who have achieved a similar goal to your own, or whose motivation and positive attitude inspires you. Find books, films or podcasts with stories of people who truly inspire you or who have suffered setbacks but persevered regardless. These stories will pick you up when you're feeling down, or remind you that everyone faces challenges along their paths but that great things can happen when you find the will to keep going.

SO MANY OF OUR DREAMS AT FIRST SEEM IMPOSSIBLE, THEN THEY SEEM IMPROBABLE, AND THEN, WHEN WE SUMMON THE WILL, THEY SOON BECOME INEVITABLE.

Christopher Reeve

WRITE A "HAVE-DONE" LIST

Do you remember how motivating it is to look back when you are walking up a hill and see all that ground you have already covered? It gives you a break from looking up at the slope to come and gives you a preview of how good it is going to feel when you reach the top. Do the same with your project.

At the end of each session you spend working toward your goal, write a "have-done" list. This is a list of everything you have achieved that day. This can be more motivating than simply crossing items off your "to-do" list. You can list the chunks of incomplete larger tasks you've worked on and recognize that progress is its own achievement, and you will see how much closer you've come to achieving your dream.

I SHALL GIVE MYSELF CREDIT WHERE CREDIT IS DUE.

THE POWER OF POSITIVE THINKING

You can be a realist and still harness the power of positive thinking. When you change the language you use to describe things, you subtly influence your own opinion of the situation. If someone asks you how your project is going, make your reply focus on the positive steps you've already taken. If you find yourself unable to do a particular task, eliminate the negative element from your thinking by changing the situation from "I can't do X so I will have to do Y or Z" to "I can do Y or Z". Tweak "disasters" to "challenges", "failures" to "learning opportunities" and view every event – positive *and* negative – as a step forward.

IF YOU'RE WALKING DOWN THE RIGHT PATH AND YOU'RE WILLING TO KEEP WALKING, EVENTUALLY YOU'LL MAKE PROGRESS.

Barack Obama

PART FOUR

FOCUS

I WILL BE
WORKING MINDFULLY,
NOT HASTILY.

The practice of mindfulness is energizing and brings clarity to your day. Practising mindfulness daily can help to create the optimum conditions for your brain to do its best work. Mindfulness is about being aware and present in the moment, focussing on the sensations you are experiencing and the environment around you. It's too easy to rush through the day, hitting bedtime before we've even really noticed what we've done. Incorporating mindfulness practices into your daily routine can help you to refocus and clear your mind of busy thoughts.

It can help to reduce stress and anxiety, two of the most common reasons people choose to give up on something. You can carve out time in your day to practise mindfulness, almost as though it were a meditation session, or you can incorporate mindfulness in your everyday activities.

If we practise mindfulness, we always have a place to be when we are afraid.

Thích Nhất Hạnh

I AM PRESENT IN THE MOMENT. I NOTICE EVERYTHING AROUND ME.

TEN MINUTES OF MINDFULNESS

If you are new to mindfulness, start small, with an easy mindfulness meditation session. Allocate ten minutes a day to practise. Find a quiet room where you will not be interrupted and sit, with your back supported. Set a ten-minute timer so you do not need to check the time during your meditation. Close your eyes and breathe slowly and deeply. Empty your mind of thoughts and focus only on your breathing; the noise you make, the sensation of the air passing your lips, the rise and fall of your chest.

If a thought intrudes, recognize it but don't follow it down a path. Think, "I have wondered what is for dinner" (for example) and return your attention to your breathing. After ten minutes, arise and return to your day.

I can create my own safe space.

MINDFULNESS IN YOUR DAILY ROUTINE

It can also be helpful to practise mindfulness during the here and now. Choose a time when your mind tends to drift, such as during the walk to the shops or while doing chores. Focus on how your senses are being engaged. So if you are walking you may note what you are seeing, such as the leaves on branches, the clouds moving in the sky, the faces of the people you pass. You may hear conversation and cars moving, with trains rumbling in the distance. There may be a smell of freshly cut grass emanating from a park that is quickly eclipsed by the smell of coffee as you pass a café. Your fingertips may be rubbing against the slightly bumpy seam of your jeans as you walk and your left big toe may be pressing against the wool of your sock.

PART FIVE

RESILIENCE

I SEE DIFFICULTIES
AS OPPORTUNITIES.

Failure doesn't have to feel bad. It doesn't reflect on the quality of person you are and it certainly isn't a reason to give up. View failure as a learning experience; every time something goes wrong, there must be a reason why. If you can discover that reason, then you can improve your process, your execution, your perspective, your environment and your knowledge, and take steps to improve for next time.

Failure is a great teacher and, if you are open to it, every mistake has a lesson to offer.

Oprah Winfrey

EVERY DAY IS THE PERFECT DAY FOR A NEW BEGINNING.

DO NOT FEAR FAILURE

A failure can feel demoralizing and lead us to stop what we are doing, thinking that if we couldn't do something this time, then we won't be able to do it ever. Tackle this by changing the conditions in which you experience failure. The next time something you try goes wrong, get out a sheet of paper and title it "What did I learn?" Write down at least one thing that you have learned from this mistake. This transforms a failure into a springboard for improving tomorrow.

I AM RESILIENT; ALTHOUGH I BEND, I DO NOT BREAK.

The roughest road often leads to the top.

Christina Aguilera

BIG ROADS HAVE BIG BUMPS

The pay-off to trying something new and challenging is a wonderful sense of achievement. It is important to accept that a natural consequence of taking such big steps is the occasional stumble. When you run into adversity, acknowledge to yourself that this is because you are trying something new. If you never try anything new, then you may not experience failure, but you would also not experience learning, achievement, wonder or world expansion. The next time you fail think to yourself, “I am doing something right.”

I DO NOT PASS
JUDGMENT
ON MYSELF.

DEALING WITH SETBACKS

On every journey, there's bound to be something that doesn't go to plan. Even small setbacks or a mid-project slump can be hard to cope with and can sometimes make us want to give everything up. This is why it's important to have coping mechanisms in place and ready to help you get back on track after an unexpected blow. Allow yourself time to work through any emotions that arise – it's perfectly normal to feel frustrated, sad or even angry, and bottling up those emotions won't do you any favours. Remind yourself that every person you now think of as successful will have experienced these setbacks, but they carried on nevertheless. If you think it will help, reach out to a trusted friend who can give you some objective feedback and help you to see how far you've come already and remind you why you're doing this in the first place. Then work out your next steps. How will you get back on track? Will you attempt the same thing again, in a different way, or is there a way around the problem area? Now put your plan into action.

I MAY FALL DOWN, BUT I ALSO BOUNCE BACK UP.

THERE IS NO MAGIC TO ACHIEVEMENT. IT'S REALLY ABOUT HARD WORK, CHOICES AND PERSISTENCE.

Michelle Obama

I have not failed. I've just found 10,000 ways that won't work.

Thomas Edison

TAKE A BREAK

Yes, this book recommends viewing failure as a positive thing that gives you valuable information for your next try, and hopefully in time you will have more of a positive than a negative reaction to any missteps on your journey. However, it's also important to recognize that this change may not come quickly.

The last thing you need is a double whammy of negativity, compounding the feeling of something going wrong with guilt that you should feel OK about this but don't. So if you're feeling down about the turn of events, it's fine to acknowledge that. Step away from your project for a while to get some space. Go for a brisk walk to create some endorphins (happy hormones), or complete a simple task to give yourself a small sense of achievement.

Never, never,
never give up.

Winston Churchill

PART SIX

MIND, BODY AND SPIRIT

I KNOW THAT MY MOST EFFECTIVE SELF IS MY HEALTHIEST SELF.

Mental fortitude is not your only source of strength. A strong, healthy body fuels a strong, healthy mind. People who eat well, sleep well and exercise regularly have better concentration and energy levels, enabling them to persevere with tasks and maintain better mental health.

Of course, you should also take care of yourself because you yourself are important, not just so that you're better able to achieve the things you set out to do. It's essential always to schedule time to attend to your needs, even if it feels like time "off".

Sleep is the golden chain that ties health and our bodies together.

Thomas Dekker

SLEEP IS PRECIOUS

Even missing just a little sleep can impact your productivity. Studies show that when you sleep less than your nightly recommended amount of 7–9 hours you experience a significant negative effect on your mood. You are more likely to feel angry, sad or stressed; none of which are going to help you persevere when things get tough.

There is good news, though – those same studies reported that when participants returned to a recommended amount of sleep, their mood improved. And you only need to "catch up" on a third of the amount of sleep missed to get back to normal – so if you've had a rough night and missed a couple of hours' sleep, a quick 30-minute nap could help to restore your energy levels.

I AM WORTH THE INVESTMENT IN MYSELF.

TIPS FOR SOUND SLEEP

If you have carved out enough time to get a healthy 7–9 hours of sleep a night but are struggling to get to sleep, or to stay asleep, then you can use a few techniques to improve this. Try using your bedroom only for sleep and for sex, so that you don't associate the room with work and other stressful things that could keep you up. Stop looking at screens at least half an hour before you go to bed and cut sugary drinks or snacks for at least an hour before bedtime. If you can, purchase a lamp with an automatic dimmer; this simulated sunset will help to draw your brain down into sleep. Have a warm bath before bed to relax you.

If you are still struggling, it's always worth seeing a doctor who can talk you through other helpful techniques and medical options.

I rest,
I recharge,
I replenish.

SOMETIMES THE MOST IMPORTANT THING IN A WHOLE DAY IS THE REST WE TAKE BETWEEN TWO DEEP BREATHS.

Etty Hillesum

OH, SUGAR!

Sugars and simple carbohydrates give us quick bursts of energy. This might seem like a good thing on the surface, but after the spike of energy comes the slump when our body has burned through the fuel. It's better to eat foods that "burn" slowly, giving us a steady, consistent source of energy throughout the day, ensuring our levels don't slump.

Ditch chocolate, sweets and crisps for nuts, fruits and vegetables. This doesn't mean you're confined to gnawing on broccoli – try slices of pepper dipped in hummus or guacamole as a mid-morning snack, or a fresh smoothie made with all your favourite fruits and some peanut butter.

MY BODY IS A MACHINE THAT NEEDS THE BEST FUEL.

EXERCISE AND ENDORPHINS

An exercise session can give you a rush of positive emotions, sometimes called a "runner's high". Some studies link this with endorphins being released as you exercise, while other studies claim that endorphins are only released after a long period of high-intensity exercise and it is more likely that you are experiencing serotonin release. Whatever the reason, it sure feels good to exercise.

When you're feeling good, it's easier to stick at things you've set your mind to. Schedule in some exercise several times a week to keep up your motivation – the World Health Organization recommends at least 150 minutes of moderate-intensity aerobic physical activity or 75 minutes of vigorous-intensity aerobic physical activity spread throughout the week to improve fitness.

PART SEVEN

TIME MANAGEMENT

THE BEST WAY TO WORK IS THE WAY THAT SUITS ME BEST.

Truly, the best way to keep at what you're doing is to enjoy it and feel stimulated by the task. You can create a short cut to feeling this positivity by working in a way that suits you, making the *how* part as efficient and simple as possible to avoid adding unnecessary extra challenges to your task.

Keep your momentum going by organizing your time according to your preference. This section explains several different techniques; experiment to find the perfect time-management arrangement for you.

Ignore the naysayers. Really the only option is, head down and focus on the job.

Chris Pine

The best way to predict your future is to create it.

Anonymous

POMODORO TECHNIQUE

No, the Pomodoro isn't a dog, it's a time-management technique. Devised in the 1980s by Francesco Cirillo, a software engineer and consultant, the technique combines short sharp bursts of working with regular breaks. The intervals are designed to improve focus during your working minutes and ensure you replenish your energy during your breaks.

The original Pomodoro technique consists of 25 minutes working followed by a five-minute break. Repeat this four times, and then take a longer break of up to 30 minutes, before starting again. This can be adapted for your own working needs – you may need longer to get into a task or work best in very short bursts – as long as the basic structure of four regular periods of work and short breaks followed by one longer break is preserved.

NOW I HAVE SET THE GOAL I CAN BUILD THE PATH TOWARD IT.

DO THE LITTLE THINGS FIRST

If you are feeling moored by indecisiveness and a too-big list of things that need to get done, netting a couple of easy wins might help to steer you away from the urge to quit. Many time-management methods advocate completing the quickest items first; the momentum of success can propel you forward and the burden of having lots to do will be lightened.

You can use the ABCD method mentioned earlier in this book to help you get started, or else simply jot down a list of everything you need to do and pick a job you know won't take long to do first. The satisfaction of ticking it off will give you a confidence boost and get you in the "productive" mindset to tackle something bigger (or another small task) next.

WHEN I ENJOY MY WORK, IT FLOURISHES.

EAT THE FROG

A (sadly apocryphal) story tells of how Mark Twain advocated eating a live frog every morning, because after that, nothing in the day could possibly be so bad. Most people who talk about "eating the frog first" don't actually recommend eating a real frog, but the metaphor of tackling your biggest and most unpleasant or daunting task first thing to get your day off to a flying start is one that works for a lot of people. It's the opposite of the "little things" approach, so you'll probably find one or the other works much better for you. The benefit of this approach is that it takes any pressure off picking which tasks to do – you *must* get on with the biggest (and often toughest) one first. But once you've tackled that, surely the rest of your work time can only be better. And you'll get an enormous boost from having stopped that big job looming over your head.

As long as I have passion, I have the fuel to achieve my goals.

DON'T BREAK THE CHAIN

Humans like rewards, even when they're intangible and don't really "mean" anything (see the incredibly successful methods most apps and video games adopt to keep you coming back for more). At the end of every day that you have worked on your project, make a mark on your calendar. Make it easily visible – you could colour the day in green, for example, or put a big tick against it. You'll not only experience the intrinsic reward of having worked on your project but you'll also enjoy the extrinsic motivation that comes from creating a "streak" or a chain of productive days. Soon you'll find yourself motivated by maintaining the chain as well as working on your endeavour.

IT'S NOT THAT I'M SO SMART; IT'S JUST THAT I STAY WITH PROBLEMS LONGER.

Albert Einstein

MY MIND IS

OPEN TO NEW

POSSIBILITIES.

BLOCK BUILDER

Be specific about what a task will entail and break that down into its own mini to-do list. Draw a large box divided into a series of blocks. Starting from the bottom, write each stage and at the top write the task itself. Cross off or colour in each block as you complete each stage, eventually crossing off the top block when the whole task is complete.

The blocks are a nice visual that work in a similar way to the "don't break the chain" method, but this approach also has the advantage of breaking every task you have into visible and digestible steps. It is easier to know where to start and how to continue, and not get lost in the details, when you have created a map for yourself.

Every step
toward my goal
is a step in the
right direction,
no matter
how small.

GET CREATIVE

Our motivation, and therefore our will not to quit, can be improved in every scenario by applying a little creativity. Creativity is the ability to link ideas in an unusual way, generate new ideas and solve problems in an unexpected manner. Those things are powerful tools in anyone's belt, even if you assumed your project didn't have a creative element.

Get your creative juices flowing by engaging creatively with the world around you. Visit an art gallery, take a photo a day, listen to a new album every week, try cooking some new recipes. Simply break out of your comfort zone for a little while and see how it inspires you.

When you come to a roadblock, take a detour.

Mary Kay Ash

DO IT STRAIGHT AWAY

The "do it straight away" approach takes the idea of prioritizing the little things one step further. The concept is that if something takes five minutes or less, do it straight away. This keeps fiddly items off your to-do list and ensures you keep up momentum while working. It's not one for the easily distracted, but it works well for those who get overwhelmed by long lists or find it hard to prioritize.

I AM ALWAYS
MOVING
FORWARD.

Problems are not stop signs, they are guidelines.

Robert H. Schuller

DAYDREAM

A study published in *Psychological Science* showed that when two groups completed a series of tasks, the group that had taken a break to let their thoughts drift were more productive than those who had taken a break to complete a challenging puzzle. Remember that quality of work is more important than quantity of work and aim to build in 5–10 minutes of daydreaming for every hour of work. You should return to your work refreshed and better able to focus on the tasks ahead.

MIX 'N' MATCH

You may have found that one of the time-management techniques listed in this book is the perfect solution to all of your motivation and discipline woes. If so, fantastic! You may discover that in fact, tweaking the premises and combining different techniques is the best way forward for you. This is still fantastic. The most important thing about any time-management technique is that it is effective in helping you to manage your time; it only need be a framework to help you find the best method for you.

Perhaps you like the Pomodoro technique but need a little extra time to get your teeth into the task. Perhaps you find the block builder process helps you to approach tasks but you need the "don't break the chain" method to keep your motivation up. Perfecting time-management techniques is all about trial and error, and there's no right or wrong way to work – as you learn what works best for you, you'll naturally fall into your own best way of working, even if it's nothing like anyone else's!

MY ENTHUSIASM AND MY POTENTIAL HAVE NO LIMIT.

I HAVE THE WILL. NOW I WILL FIND THE WAY.

Imagination is the beginning of creation.

George Bernard Shaw

Do one thing every day that scares you.

Eleanor Roosevelt

PART EIGHT

POSITIVE THINKING

I DESERVE TO
TREAT MYSELF KINDLY
AND GENTLY.

It really is true: if you believe it, then you can achieve it. People who believe in themselves are far less likely to give up on themselves than those who are constantly plagued by self-doubt. Their road is clearer; they only have to overcome the obstacles in their path rather than first battling obstacles they've placed in their own way.

You do your best work when you are your best self. Here are a few techniques to help you build self-esteem, so that you'll be ready to give your all to your project.

BE BRAVE ENOUGH TO
BE YOUR TRUE SELF.

Queen Latifah

POSITIVITY CAN SHINE A LIGHT THROUGH CLOUDS OF WORRY.

BE YOURSELF

Strong self-esteem stems from your own good opinion of yourself. It can't be built on the foundations of other people's opinions of you or how you judge yourself in comparison to others. The only person whose achievements you should compare your own with is your past self. True confidence stems from trusting your own judgment, being able to recognize and celebrate your own strengths, to identify your weaknesses and not berate yourself over them, and to feel fear but not let it get in your way.

If you find yourself comparing your achievements and attributes with other people's, then stop your train of thought. Mentally "walk away" from that way of thinking and remind yourself that you must judge yourself on your own merits.

AFFIRMATIONS

Affirmations really do help magic self-esteem into being. It's a simple hack for your brain; humans respond well to repetition. Once a day, at an easily remembered time, such as when you clean your teeth, repeat an affirmation to yourself – in your head, or out loud if you like (though maybe not while brushing your teeth!). Repeat it several times, and really think about the power behind the words. It should be short, pithy and positive, targeting the areas you feel you need to boost. Try one of these, or make up your own:

1. **I am capable of everything I try.**
2. **Today is going to be a good day.**
3. **I am a strong, productive person.**

I pledge to treat myself kindly, to support my own choices and to silence any doubting voices.

WE MUST
ACCEPT FINITE
DISAPPOINTMENT
BUT WE MUST NEVER
LOSE INFINITE HOPE

Martin Luther King Jr

KEEP A TRIGGER DIARY

Sometimes part of discovering how to improve something is learning what is making it go wrong in the first place. Investigate whether there is anything triggering negative emotions and loss of self-confidence in your life. Keep a daily diary for two weeks, noting down everything you do and recording your mood as you do it. Analyse your mood patterns and see if there is anything in particular that is triggering your more negative moods. Perhaps it's taking a certain journey, performing a task or even seeing a certain person.

From there you can work out a strategy; ideally to stop engaging in whatever is bringing you down or to reduce your engagement with it, but if you must continue, you'll have an advantage in knowing the dip is coming and being able to fortify yourself mentally.

IF I FALL DOWN,
THEN I WILL
EXTEND MYSELF
A HAND AND GET
BACK UP AGAIN.

TACKLE ANXIETY

Anxiety disorders can be tricky to spot, as they are defined by normal emotions, such as sadness or worry, but they are magnified to an extreme level. Some anxiety disorders can cause the sufferer to think badly about themselves, to judge their efforts harshly and sometimes to imagine that their friends and family share in this negative opinion of them. If your project or your everyday life has become negatively impacted by low self-esteem, worry and stress then first visit your GP – there are resources and treatment plans available to help you, and looking after your mental health should be your number one priority.

I AM MY OWN SHELTER AGAINST THE STORM.

LIFE SHRINKS
OR EXPANDS IN
PROPORTION TO
ONE’S COURAGE.

Anaïs Nin

ACKNOWLEDGE COMPLIMENTS

Resist the urge to brush off compliments you receive. Reply with "thank you" and make the conscious decision to believe what the person has said to you. Remember the good things that have been said to you – if you need reminding, then set up a page in your diary or notebook. Write down the compliments that you receive, especially those about elements of yourself that you have control over, such as your style, personality and achievements. When you are having a day when you feel badly about yourself, return to that page and look at the evidence that you are valued and appreciated.

I STRIVE TO BE THE BEST VERSION OF MYSELF; I DO NOT COMPARE MYSELF TO OTHERS.

DODGE NEGATIVE VIBES

We are all affected by our environment. Sometimes that environment includes people. Perhaps you've noticed, using the diary technique mentioned earlier in the book, that interacting with a certain person generates negative feelings. This can be because the other person is verbalizing a lot of worries of their own – when you are already feeling stressed it's easy to absorb the feelings you're discussing, which in turn makes it harder to distinguish between your own worries and those of others. It may make sense to draw back from that relationship for a time while you fortify your mental health.

Caring for myself is not self-indulgence, it is self-preservation.

Audre Lorde

I acknowledge negative thoughts I have about myself and I let them go.

THINK SOLUTIONS

When worry and self-doubt are getting on top of you and bringing you close to quitting, have this question in your back pocket: "What am I going to do about it?" Thinking through a problem logically is useful when you first encounter it; it allows you to work through what has happened and form a plan to solve it. Dwelling on negative emotions too much without finding a way to move forward is unhelpful. If you find yourself falling into this pattern, ask yourself instead what your solution is.

If you've already planned for all possible contingencies, acknowledge that you are wasting your time and emotions by worrying, and let the thoughts go.

Self-trust is the first secret of success.

Ralph Waldo Emerson

PART NINE

SUCCESS

HALF THE BATTLE
IS KNOWING
WHEN I'VE WON.

At the beginning of the book we recommended that you write down clear and achievable goals. It is important to recognize when you have achieved those goals. After all, this is what you're aiming for. Set aside time to celebrate yourself; you will feel energized and your self-esteem will receive a boost.

Act as if what you do makes a difference. It does.

William James

I GIVE MYSELF PERMISSION TO CELEBRATE MY ACHIEVEMENTS.

CELEBRATE, BUT KEEP ON

The completion of any goal should be celebrated. In many cases it's the result of your long, hard work. Not only is that an achievement worth celebrating, but marking the occasion can help you to keep moving forward. If your project is the kind without a clear "end", such as learning a new language, then you should still take the time to mark your successes. It's easy to feel like you're not making progress when you're working on a continuous task, and that can be demoralizing. Taking time out to appreciate what you've done so far will help you to keep up the momentum to carry on, and give you an incentive to keep progressing even further still.

I DIDN'T **QUIT,**
AND IT WAS
WORTH IT.

CONGRATULATIONS!

If, on the other hand, your goal did have a clear end point, and you've reached it – congratulations! Of course, the main thing to do at this point is to celebrate what you have achieved, and maybe give yourself some time off to relax and reflect on your accomplishment. Your hard work has paid off. But perhaps this doesn't have to be the end? Are there any ways you can magnify the effects of your achievements? Can you help to inspire others by sharing your story? Could you create a new, even more ambitious goal, to maintain the momentum? Think about where you want to go from here and how you might continue your winning streak.

Opportunities multiply as they are seized.

Sun Tzu

FALL DOWN
SEVEN TIMES,
STAND UP EIGHT.

Japanese proverb

CONCLUSION

DON'T QUIT, DO IT

I WILL ENJOY THE POWER THAT COMES FROM PURSUING MY DREAMS.

Whether your intention was to overhaul your life or just break that one bad habit, you should now be well-equipped to start, continue and see your endeavours all the way to success. Hopefully the suggestions in this book will continue to help you even after you've reached your goal, and in other areas of your life. Having the skills to keep yourself motivated and to build your self-esteem and resilience are gifts that keep on giving – you should experience the cycle of confidence that comes with working well, knowing what suits you and achieving your dreams. We wish you every luck on your journey to success, and remember: you've got this!

I WILL
NOT QUIT.

SUCCESS IS NOT FINAL,
FAILURE IS NOT FATAL:
IT IS THE COURAGE
TO CONTINUE THAT
COUNTS.

Winston Churchill

If you're interested in finding out more about our books, find us on Facebook at **Summersdale Publishers** and follow us on Twitter at **@Summersdale**.

www.summersdale.com

Image credits